PEVENSEY &
1900 - 2000

A CENTURY OF CHANGE

A portrait of the area
in old and new photographs

David Brook

S.B. Publications

By the same author:
Pevensey, Westham and District,
A Portrait in Old Picture Postcards (1992)

First published in 2000 by S.B. Publications
19 Grove Road, Seaford,
East Sussex BN25 1TP

ISBN 1 85770 218 2

Typeset and printed by
Tansleys The Printers
19 Broad Street, Seaford, East Sussex BN25 1LS
Telephone: (01323) 891019

CONTENTS

PEVENSEY

PEVENSEY BAY

FOREWORD

I was delighted when I was asked by my brother to write the foreword to this book.

Over recent years there have been numerous books produced using old postcards or photographs depicting specific areas of Sussex, which have all been of interest to local people and visitors to the area. This book is different. It is the first one I have seen, where the author has taken the trouble to go to the place where the old photograph was taken (or as near as possible) and take a new photograph of the scene and juxtapose it with the old photograph.

This is fascinating to anyone not familiar with the area, to appreciate the location and see the changes over a period of time.

I can remember, for instance, as a child, being taken to see the burnt out remains of the old "Thatched House" (see page 60) the day after the fire. Our father being a member of the local fire brigade, he had helped to fight the fire.

Being able to remember some of the old scenes myself, I am conscious not only of these changes, but how little some of the scenes have changed, except superficially, with the passing of the years.

With the current rate of progress, it will be interesting to compare these photographs with new ones in a few years time.

It must be said, that some of the changes are definitely for the better. A few of the buildings that have been demolished in the intervening years would certainly not be acceptable as living accommodation in our modern society. To have brought them up to an acceptable standard would have involved such radical changes, that the resulting building would have had only a superficial resemblance to the original.

It is only in such a book as this one, that one realises how dramatic some of the changes are. Without these photographs, who, for example would realise how much shingle has been lost from Pevensey Bay. (see page 71). Only people continually working there I suspect, and probably not all of them.

I hope this book inspires others to produce similar works of their own area, for the benefit of posterity. Fortunately, people today are becoming more aware of the loss of their local familiar surroundings. Once they are lost they are lost for ever.

Peter Brook

INTRODUCTION

For their programme for the Millennium year, the Pevensey and Westham Historical Society have compiled a series of ten illustrated talks. Each talk to illustrate the happenings of each century relating to the district over the last one thousand years.

I was privileged to be asked to prepare a talk for the last century of the Millennium and illustrate it with slides of old postcards and photographs I have amassed over the years.

Coming from this I was asked if I would be interested in selecting a series of them to make up a book to complement the one I have already had published on the area, and to use the talk to launch it to the Society and the general public.

Without the help of the many residents past and present who have given me old photos or loaned them to me to copy, this book would not have been possible, and I am indebted to them for the co-operation they have given me.

David Brook
December 2000

Front cover: **PEVENSEY CASTLE**

After being neglected for centuries and falling into disrepair, the castle was given to the nation in 1925 by His Grace the Duke of Devonshire. Since then, the fabric of the castle has gradually been renovated and the walls consolidated. The process being completed in the late 1990s.

Back cover: **HANKHAM STREET**

Much has changed from the dirt roads when children could walk carefree anywhere without fear of injury from traffic with only horse-drawn vehicles and bicycles.

GLENLEIGH MANOR
Dating from 1608, the Elizabethan farmhouse was rendered outside early in the last century when purchased by Mr Cunliffe-Smith. After a disastrous fire in the 1970s it was turned into an hotel.

LUSTEDS

Originally called Horns, the house was burnt to the ground in 1935, rebuilt in the following years and greatly extended in the 1990s.

HORNS COTTAGES

Col. Owen of the Horns had these cottages refurbished for men coming home from the First World War. The new house was built in the 1970s. *(Top Photo: Col. Owen Collection)*

TRANSPORT 1900
One of the most significant changes to our lives at the turn of the century was the change from horses to horsepower. *(Photo: Col. Owen Collection)*

HANKHAM TEA GARDENS

A popular venue for outings from Eastbourne since the turn of the century by horse carriage and motor coaches, even in the First World War when petrol was rationed and coaches were driven by coal gas.

HANKHAM BLACKSMITH'S SHOP

Mr Thorpe wearing his leather apron, stands outside his blacksmith's shop with Mr Breach, a shepherd from Prieshawes farm, holding the horses. The house with the porch was the village shop. *(Top Photo: Col. Owen Collection)*

THE DOG HOUSE

The Dog House was built c1600 and for many years it was three cottages. It was occupied by the army during the Second World War and converted into one residence soon after the end of the war.

ST. MICHAEL AND ALL ANGELS

Known as the tin chapel, because of its roof, it was de-consecrated in 1928 when Stone Cross church was built. It was demolished in the 1970s after which the new house was built.

FORGE HOUSE

Mr Geering Snr. and daughter standing in the garden of their house that stood opposite the forge at Blackness, now replaced by the modern building built in the late 1990s. *(Top Photo: Mrs Funnell)*

THE BLACKSMITH'S FORGE

The three sons of Mr Geering, all blacksmiths, standing outside the forge and travis to the right, where the horses were shod. Both buildings were demolished for the Pevensey bypass in the 1980s. *(Top Photo: Mrs Funnell)*

STONE CROSS CROSSROADS
The old tollhouse for the Horsebridge to Langney Turnpike road was demolished in the 1960s for the widening of the A27 trunk road. Stone Cross Hall was built in the 1920s. *(Top Photo: S.A.S.)*

STONE CROSS WINDMILL

The mill was built in 1876. A gale in 1928 blew off two of the sweeps but it remained in regular use until 1932. It has been fully restored for the millennium.

PEELINGS MANOR

According to old sales catalogues, a licence was granted in 1602 to build at Peelings. Over the years it has been restored with many alterations.

PEELINGS OAST HOUSES

The Oast Houses were used to dry the hops that were grown on the estate which extended up to Stone Cross crossroads. The buildings are now privately owned.

(Top Photo: S.A.S.)

FOORDS LANE

The two old cottages have been replaced by modern bungalows. The gateway to the vicarage of St. Michael's church, Hankham is on the left.

PEVENSEY BYPASS

In the 1980s, the much needed A27 bypass was constructed. The pictures taken from Hankham Hall road, show the construction and the finished road towards Pevensey.

GALLOWS LANE CROSSROADS

Known as Ketcham Corner, from the days when Excise men waited here for gangs of up to 100 smugglers from Pevensey Bay going towards Hailsham.

THE ALMSHOUSES

The Almshouses belong to St. John's Trust. The top photograph shows the building which replaced the original thatched Almshouses. The modern Almshouses were built in the 1970s. *(Top Photo: J. Wootton)*

THE GONDOLA LAKE
Formed when the clay for the brickworks was dug out for the building of the Victorian houses in Westham. It was filled in and built over with a housing estate in the 1970s.

WESTHAM STATION

The Victorian waiting room, steam engines, stationmaster and ten staff have given way to automatic ticket machines and digital clocks.

WESTHAM CROSSROADS

The Railway Hotel with its large car park and gardens was demolished in the 1970s and the present terrace of houses built in its place. *(Top Photo: L. Backler)*

EASTBOURNE PLEASURE BOATS

For those of you who have taken "a trip around the lighthouse" at Eastbourne, how many of you realised that they were built in a barn in Westham. *(Top Photo: E. Hoare)*

STREET FARM BARN

The barn stood opposite the chemist shop, one of two belonging to the farm. The other one stood in the field by the pond, now garages for Montfort Close.

(Top Photo: P. Brook)

CHRISTMAS, c1950s

If you took a parcel to the paper shop in the village and paid one shilling, you could have it delivered by the British Legion on Christmas Day by stagecoach.

(Top Photo: C. E.. Smith)

STREET FARMHOUSE

The farmhouse, with its front porch and garden railings, stood out on the corner of High Street and Peelings Lane. Today, its original position is occupied by the pavement as shown in the lower picture, in the left foreground.

THE HORSE POND AND BLACKSMITH'S FORGE

The barn and farm were demolished and the road straightened when the new estates were built. The old blacksmith's shop is now a coppersmith.

THE OLD BAKER'S SHOP

Now a private dwelling, the baker's shop had its own bread oven in the back and was also the village Post Office, later to become one of the village butchers.

(Top Photo: Col. Owen Collection, Bottom Photo: P. Brook)

PEVENSEY CASTLE HOTEL

The livery stables have been replaced by a car park and Myrtle cottages by flats.
Parking on the pavement has always been a problem.

WESTHAM HIGH STREET
High Street at the turn of the century, with its barber shop and hairdressers. The shop at the end was used for the collection of harnesses for repair by Larkins of Hailsham.

WESTHAM SHOPS

Barnes, butchers and Keene and Morgan, drapers and outfitters, have been changed to a private house and King's, newsagent.

CHURCH FARM AND NEWSAGENTS

Photographed on Election Day 1908, outside the farmyard of Church Farm, when Beaumont, standing as a radical, was elected for Eastbourne. *(Top Photo: Col. Owen Collection)*

EDWARD VII's CORONATION

The whole of the village took part in the celebration with the street dressed overall and a parade with a church service to follow. *(Top Photo: Col. Owen Collection)*

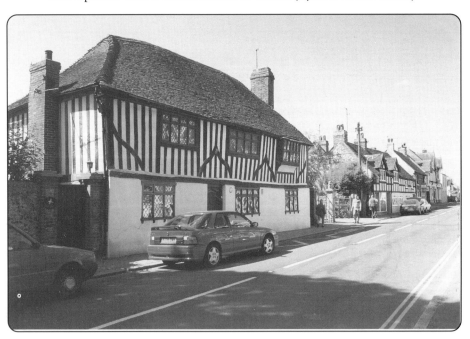

WESTHAM STREET, LOOKING WEST

Before the era of the motor car, the street, with Church Farm on the left and very little curbing, was a much quieter place than today with the modern traffic.

INTERIOR, WESTHAM CHURCH
The top photograph shows the interior with its oil lamps. The rood screen was repositioned in 1913 after standing for many years at the rear of the church.

WESTHAM CHURCH AND GRAVEYARD

A view taken from the south east before the churchyard was extended into the field to the south of the church.

THE OLD BUTCHER'S SHOP

This stood at the east end of High Street with an abattoir at the rear. It became a grocer's shop during the first quarter of the century. It is now a private dwelling.

WESTHAM CHURCH

A last view of Westham looking from the Roman west gateway with the church visible before the trees obscured the view today. *(Top Photo: Col. Owen Collection)*

IVY COTTAGE TEA ROOMS
A popular place to take tea in the afternoon, it was demolished in the late 1950s along with all the out buildings.

CASTLE ROAD

Before its restoration much of the castle was covered in ivy. The window in the tower was filled in when it was used as a gun emplacement during the Second World War.

THE ELIZABETHAN CANNON
The cannon has now been moved to the inner castle and a gun carriage made for it.
The outline of the original gun emplacement is now marked by a plaque.

NORMAN INTERIOR OF CASTLE
The Eagle Tower was full of debris before restoration and the entrance to the drawbridge half covered over.

THE NORMAN KEEP

The keep as it was when it was given to the nation. Approximately 1.2 metres have
been removed from the ground of the inner castle and all the trees and debris
removed from the keep.

THE NORMAN CASTLE

The Norman Eagle and north towers have been much restored and the drawbridge replaced, a favourite place to sit and reflect on times past.

CHURCH LANE, PEVENSEY

The old cattle market and its market office, shown lower right foreground, is now occupied by a car park. At this time the churchyard had not been extended and was still used as an orchard to the farm.

THE ROMAN EAST GATE

Showing the entrance as it was with its eleven steps into the castle. Cycling was a popular recreation in the 1920s, as it is today.

THE OLD MINTHOUSE

Originally three cottages, the centre one was "The little shop" at the turn of the century, later to become a museum and antique shop.

THE MARKET SQUARE

The square, the original market, no longer has sheep driven over it to be sold at the market. It is now used as a car park for the many visitors throughout the year.

(Top Photo: V. Murray)

THE CATTLE MARKET
There had been a cattle market at Pevensey for many centuries and cattle used to come by train to Westham and be driven to the market round the castle.

THE ROYAL OAK

Standing on the edge of the market square, the owners used to have to pay rent for their porch and garden railings as they were built on Pevensey Town Trust land.

THE OLD FARMHOUSE

When looking at the roof and chimney one can see that the building has been enlarged to the east. Old postcards show it as one of the many tea-rooms.

THE OLD COURTHOUSE AND BUTCHER'S SHOP
Reputed to be the smallest Town Hall in England with its jail underneath, it is now a museum. The butcher's shop, shown in the centre of the top photograph, had its own abattoir at the rear.

THE NEW INN

Now The Smugglers, The New Inn was named because it was moved from the south
side of the road to the north. Pevensey fire engine was originally housed there.

ENTRANCE TO PEVENSEY CASTLE

Before restoration and the replacement of the drawbridge, the only access to the inner castle was from the steps at the tearooms on the east side of the castle.

PEVENSEY CHURCH

Greatly restored in 1870 when the tower was heightened from the course of bricks below the louvres. The clock was installed in 1908.

HIGH STREET, PEVENSEY

Showing the New Inn on the right and Penthouse Cottages on the left.
The square building on the left used to be the village Post Office.

PEVENSEY FIRE APPLIANCE

The original horse-drawn appliance was bought from Eastbourne at the turn of the century. All the firemen wore brass helmets and the pump was manually driven by the handles on the sides.

PEVENSEY BRIDGE

Until 1390 when the bridge was built, the only way across was by ferry. All the
sheep from Pevensey marsh were brought here for their annual dipping.

CHILLEY BRIDGE AND PYLONS
The pylons were one of a series built along the South Coast for radar detection of enemy aircraft in the Second World War. They were first used on Good Friday, 1939.

CHILLEY FARM
The Plumley family have been farming here for over three hundred years. The course of time has taken its toll on the barn and modern innovations such as electricity have been installed. *(Top Photo: Col. Owen Collection)*

THE OLD THATCH
A thatched restaurant replaced this old cottage in the 1930s, which was set on fire while occupied by the army in the 1940s. The modern houses were built in the 1970s.

FENCE BRIDGE

The white bungalow on the bridge was built as a tea house with the old thatch in the background. The river was realigned in 1979 because of road subsidence.

PEVENSEY LEVEL CROSSING

With no pavement and only dirt roads it must have been very dusty in the summer and wet and muddy in the winter if travelling on foot. *(Top Photo: Col. Owen Collection)*

PEVENSEY BAY CROSSROADS

Now a newsagent, the shop was originally a dairy and post office. The house on the beach was demolished by a bomb during the Second World War. *(Top Photo: Col. Owen Collection)*

THE OLD FISHERMANS COTTAGES
Standing on the north side of Richmond Road, the cottages are reputed to be over three hundred years old.

THE BAY HOTEL
Built in the late 1880s, the wooden veranda has now been removed. The white pinnacle on the top has been used as a fishing marker to find a selected site ever since it was built.

ST. WILFRED'S HALL

Built in 1881 as a church and hall, it was demolished when the new church was
built between Collier Road and Bay Road.

MARTELLO TOWER 61

Erected in 1805 when the threat from Napoleon was imminent, the tower was then used by the Excise to combat smuggling. All Martello Towers had a cannon on the roof. It is now a private dwelling.

NORTH EAST VIEW FROM TOWER 61
The old fisherman's cottages can be seen in Richmond Road, which was a
cul-de-sac, with the twitten leading to Collier Road.

SOUTH WEST VIEW FROM TOWER 61
As can be seen, the beach today has only four towers remaining looking towards Langney Point, with considerable development on the beach towards Langney.

MARTELLO TOWER, GRENVILLE ROAD
Tower 62 was used as an observation post in the Second World War, isolated but now surrounded by flats and houses.

THE BEACH, LEYLAND ROAD
Beach erosion has always been a problem which has become more serious over the years. The continual battle against the sea goes on

VIEW TO LANGNEY POINT
Only three towers remain in bottom picture. The wooden groynes erected to stop the erosion of the beach do nothing for the landscape.

THE LIDO
Standing on the beach at the top of Sea Road, this was a popular cafe before the Second World War. It became derelict and was replaced by the Beach Tavern.

RED HOUSE FARM
For many years this was the eastern boundary of Pevensey Bay. The Red Cross hall was built in the late 1960s.